Ehlang, Erin, Author
The Feelings Book

ISBN: 979-8-9927928-1-2
ISBN: 979-8-9927928-0-5
ISBN: 979-8-9927928-2-9
ISBN: 979-8-9927928-3-6
ISBN: 979-8-9927928-4-3

FAM016000   FAMILY & RELATIONSHIPS / Education
FAM025000   FAMILY & RELATIONSHIPS / Life Stages / Infants & Toddlers

QUANTITY PURCHASES: Schools, companies, professional groups, clubs,
and other organizations may qualify for special terms when ordering quantities of this title.

For information, email mrs.ehlang@gmail.com

Feelings are felt in your body and heart.
Some feelings feel good,
which is the best part!

Bad feelings feel like they last and they last,
but always remember, that soon
they will pass.

Happy can look like smiles and joy!
Like laughing with friends or playing with toys.

Enjoy when you're happy, and share it with friends. I hope that happy for you never ends!

Sad hurts in your heart and might make you cry, you may feel sad when you have to say goodbye.

Hugs are good medicine for sad, did you know?
Hug someone close to you, long, tight, and slow.

Excited can make it feel very hard to wait, for something that seems so fun and so great!

Being patient takes time,
you might hum a tune,
what you are waiting for
will come very soon.

Mad is anger, you might not know why,
You may want to throw something or sit
down and cry.

When you feel mad it's important to share,
your thoughts and your feelings with
someone who cares.

Curious is wondering why? and how?
How do things work? I want to know now!

I want to know why the stars
shine bright at night.
I have an idea,
I hope that I'm right!

Calm and peaceful make your body feel quiet.
Like relaxing at home, it's great! You should try it.

When you are calm, your brain feels more clear,
to read or talk with the people who are near.

Scared can be fear, anxiety or doubt. Take a belly breath, then let it all out.

The more breaths you take the better
you'll feel, then your scared feeling
will not seem so real.

Love is simply the best feeling of all.
Tell someone you love them, give them a call.

Love builds us up and makes our hearts feel warm.
Appreciate all love, it comes in many forms.

Feelings make our body have good and bad days.

It is okay to have feelings in all kinds of ways.

Feelings make you human, they come and they go,
the more feelings you feel, the more you will grow.

Everybody has a choice when they have a feeling.
What you choose to do gives life its meaning.

Do the right thing and you'll know right away
That no matter what you feel it will all be okay.